GOLF GREENS of IRELAND

a nostalgic look

by
John Hanna

FORE! word

As we enter the third millennium golf in Ireland is an extremely popular game enjoyed by an increasing number of Irish people and by golfing addicts from around the world who come to savour the delights of the numerous courses throughout the island, especially on our famous links courses.

This popularity has itself led to a growing interest in the origins and history of the game in Ireland and how it became an established sport around the middle of the nineteenth century. This marvellous collection of pictures adds an important pictorial record to the history of the development of the game. Some of the earlier courses featured here have ceased to exist, while some have changed their names or moved from their original site and most have brand new modern clubhouses. For example, after nearly one hundred years the clubhouse at Lahinch (page 24) is rather different today, whereas 'The Dell', the sixth hole, is still the same as it was when designed by Alister Mackenzie. While standing on the first tee at Royal County Down with the picture on page 39 in your hand, you would see that not much has changed, although the tee was further back in 1914.

John Hanna is a member of the British Golf Collectors Society and a recent winner of their President's Prize for his contribution to the society. He is a well-known authority on the history of golf and, revealing my own antiquity, I have known him for forty years. I commend this excellent book to all enthusiasts of Irish golfing and know that they will find it both interesting and enjoyable.

William G. Black
President, Golfing Union of Ireland

© John Hanna, 2002
First published in the United Kingdom, 2002,
by Stenlake Publishing,
Telephone / Fax: 01290 551122

ISBN 1 84033 187 9

THE PUBLISHERS REGRET THAT THEY CANNOT SUPPLY
COPIES OF ANY PICTURES FEATURED IN THIS BOOK.

FURTHER READING

The books listed below were used by the author during his research. None of them are available from Stenlake Publishing. Those interested in finding out more are advised to contact their local bookshop or reference library.

Geoffrey S. Cornish and Ronald E. Whitten, *The Golf Course*, Windward, 1981.
William H. Gibson, *Early Irish Golf*, Oakleaf, 1988.
William A. Menton, *The Golfing Union of Ireland*, Gill and Macmillan, 1991.
John Redmond, *The Book of Irish Golf*, Gill and Macmillan, 1997.
The Golfer's Handbook (various editions)

You can easily arrange a Match at PORTRUSH.

THE GAME OF GOLF. A Close Match.

Over the last century lady golfers have always been part of the golfing scene in Ireland. They played an important part in the development of many golf clubs, and like their male counterparts, they founded their own union, the Irish Ladies' Golf Union, in 1893. The Killymoon Golf Club staged the first open ladies' competition in May 1891. Mixed foursomes golf has always been a popular format, and many 'close matches' flourished beyond the links.

INTRODUCTION

Historians continue to argue over the origins of the game of golf. The game, as we know it today, can be more easily traced to its early beginnings in Scotland. However there are those who, having looked at Scotland's early trading partner, are more ready to say that golf had its start as a winter sport on the icy canals of the Netherlands. A favourite pastime of the Dutch was the game of 'Kolf' or 'Kolven' where a ball was struck at a post set in the ice, using just one club. A similar game was sometimes also played on the ground. There is no evidence, however, that there was a hole in the ground. Whatever its origins, many golfers will be surprised to read that golf has been around for some time. As early as the 1400s James II of Scotland was banning 'gowf', as it was called, because as a pastime it was interfering with the more serious archery practice. Archery, after all, was necessary for national defence.

There is no mention of golf in England until the seventeenth century when James VI of Scotland succeeded to the throne as James I of England. He took his courtiers to Blackheath where the English began to play golf. By the eighteenth century clubs and societies were being formed, the first being the Gentleman Golfers of Leith in 1734. When they moved from Leith Links their name changed to the Honourable Company of Edinburgh Golfers. It was this group which drew up the first Rules of Golf. Although there were only thirteen rules, they formed the basis of the Rules of Golf as they exist today.

In 1744 the Society of St Andrew's Golfers was formed. In 1834 King William IV became the Society's patron and conferred upon it the title of the Royal and Ancient Golf Club of St Andrews. This club is the headquarters of the game for most of the world in co-operation with the United States Golf Association.

Early Irish Golf by William H. Gibson is the authoritative work on the history of golf in Ireland. He states that the earliest mention of golf in this country was in 1606 when, at the time of the Plantation of Ulster, two Scots settled in a part of the Ards Peninsula. They included in their development a green 'for the recreation of goff'. No record exists of golf being played here, but records do show that golf was played at Bray as early as 1762. Golf was also played at the Curragh in 1852. However it was in Belfast where the first club was formed in 1881, later becoming the Royal Belfast Golf Club. This is accepted as being the oldest golf club in Ireland.

It is also widely recognised that the early development of golf in Ireland, as in many other parts of the world, was due to the presence of British Army Regiments, particularly Scottish ones. With the advent of the railways, coupled with increased leisure time for working people, the expansion of the game of golf became much more widespread. Many of the first golf courses were sited at the seaside resorts to which the railways travelled. Many courses relied upon the railways and their associated hotels for financial help, both in the development of the courses and for the sponsorship of competitions. The railway companies often supplied the early trophies. The seaside also provided the natural home of true links courses, which permitted play throughout the year. Summer golf was not possible in inland courses, where the grass grew too quickly and could not be cut. This was before the advent of more sophisticated grass cutting machinery.

Much of this early development of golf took place just before and after the turn of the century. Postcards were then the favourite medium for short messages and were often delivered locally on the same day. Collecting postcards showing all sorts of subjects was also a popular pastime and as a result early cards can still be found in excellent condition. While there is not room to include pictures of every Irish club, this book collects some of the best Irish golfing cards together for the first time and it is hoped that the collection will give a valuable and fascinating insight into Irish golf's early years.

Adare Manor, left, is one of two golf courses in the pretty village of Adare in County Limerick. This clubhouse set back amongst some magnificent trees is on the earlier of the two courses which was laid out by Ben Sayers as a private course for Lord Dunraven. It was started in 1898, but instituted as a club in September 1900. The Adare Golf Club is a modern course designed by Robert Trent Jones Snr and is laid out in the grounds of the Adare Manor Hotel.

Situated along the cliffs above the County Down fishing village, Ardglass Golf Club came into being in 1896. Foremost among the group responsible was the Presbyterian minister for Ardglass, the Reverend Thomas Macafee. Originally laid out as seven holes only, it was extended to nine holes very shortly after its opening. It was not until 1971 that it became eighteen. This card posted in 1925 depicts a group driving to the first hole, while another group is standing on the eighth, or sundial hole. The sundial was part of the original estate, owned by Aubrey De vere Beauclerk, on which the course was built.

The Pavilion, Arklow Golf Club.

Here is a typical view of a group of golfers, both men and women, on the first tee below the fine wooden clubhouse at Arklow Golf Club in County Wicklow. This club was formed in 1927 and now has an eighteen hole course, with the added interest of having to play over several sea inlets.

This wonderful postcard, posted in 1905, illustrates the early relationship between hotels and the development of golf. Some 100 years later the same relationship exists. A private course, the Atlantic Golf Links at Kilbrittain never became affiliated to the Golfing Union of Ireland. Established in 1902, it was listed in the *Golfing Annual* as the Kilbrittain Golf Course. The course appears to have been built on sloping land and the difficulties of playing can clearly be seen. Caddies were obviously necessary. This County Cork course disappeared, like many others, in 1916, presumably a victim of the political changes occurring in the country at that time.

CHAMPIONSHIP GOLF AT BALLYBUNION

Ballybunion golf course in County Kerry is a world-renowned championship links course which was instituted in 1896. James McKenna, professional at Lahinch, laid out the course, the cost being met by the Lartigue Railway Company. The course was extended to eighteen holes in 1926. Ten years later Tom Simpson remodelled the course prior to the Irish Close Championship. This was the first of three Irish championships won by the legendary Jimmy Bruen. He was just sixteen years of age. The postcard shows the final of the Irish Ladies' Championship of 1936 when Clarrie Tiernan beat Miss S. Moore by seven and six.

Ballycastle has always been a popular seaside resort on the north Antrim coast. One of the earliest in Ireland, the golf course was founded in 1891 mainly due to the influence of Commander Causton R.N. who was divisional officer of the local coastguard. It was one of the nine founding clubs of the Golfing Union of Ireland, the oldest golfing union in the world. This postcard, posted in September 1906, shows a mixed group driving from the Ladies' Tee at the Tennis or fourth hole.

Valentines Series

Bangor is a popular seaside resort on the coast of north Down. The golf club there was founded in 1903 and the clubhouse in the postcard was built in 1904. The original nine holes were extended to eighteen two years later. After land, which included the above clubhouse, was sold and additional land purchased, the present course was laid out by the great Open champion James Braid in 1932. The course was remodelled later by P. Mackenzie Ross.

Golf Links, Birr.

When this County Offaly Club was formed in 1893 it was known as the King's County and Ormonde Golf Club. Originally a nine-hole course close to Birr Station, sometime between 1911 and 1914 it moved to its present site at The Glens, became eighteen holes and changed its name to Birr Golf Club. When constructed the new course had one hole of 520 yards which even now would be considered a long hole. With hickory shafted clubs it would have been a very long one, especially if wearing a stiff collar on one's shirt, as is worn by the gentleman on the right.

This card was posted in 1908 and gives a good idea of the golfing dress of the time. The closeness of the course to the town can also be seen. Golf in Bray, County Wicklow, is written about as early as 1762, when links were played on by members of the Honourable Company of Edinburgh Golfers serving in the Royal Scots Regiment. However, it was 1897 before Bray Golf Club was formed. The course remains a nine-hole course in County Wicklow. A move to an eighteen-hole course may be imminent.

Golf Club House and Links, Castlerock

Castlerock is a fine seaside links course on the north coast of County Derry. It was established in 1901 and the original nine-hole course was laid out by James Coburn who was the professional at Royal Portrush. The clubhouse in the postcard was burnt down in 1913, a fate which befell many wooden clubhouses. The course was extended to eighteen holes in 1908 and now has twenty-seven holes.

CLONMEL GOLF LINKS.   R.28

Clonmel Golf Club, set in the foothills of the Comeragh Mountains in County Tipperary, was founded in 1911. Judging by the size of the gallery, this must have been quite an important match. The course has eighteen holes with a mountain stream coming into play on a number of holes. As can be seen there are many scenic views from the course.

The County Louth Golf Club (right), otherwise known as Baltray, is another fine links course on the east coast of County Louth. The formation of the club dates back to 1892 when it began as a nine-hole course. By 1894 it had been extended to eighteen holes. Cecil Barcroft, secretary of the Royal Dublin Club, redesigned the course in 1914 and it was modernised in 1938 by the famous golf architect partnership of Tom Simpson and Molly Gourlay. Baltray is the home of the annual East of Ireland Championship which began in 1941. The legendary amateur golfer Joe Carr of Sutton won this championship in its inaugural year and a further eleven times between 1943 and 1969. His son, Roddy Carr, won it in 1970. The clubhouse also had bedrooms for visiting golfers.

Rosses Point is the name commonly given to the County Sligo Golf Club. Founded in 1894, this club, like many others, owed its existence to the efforts of a highly influential, charismatic figure, in this case Lieutenant Colonel James Campbell, assisted by the local Freemason's lodge. Colonel Campbell laid out the first nine holes. These were extended to eighteen holes in 1907, designed by the Colonel's younger stepbrother, Captain Willie Campbell. Home of the West of Ireland Championship since 1923, it was soon realised that the course needed radical upgrading. In 1927 the club decided to employ the most celebrated golf course architect of the period, H.S. Colt, and Rosses Point is one of his highly acclaimed links courses, which also include Rosapenna and Royal Portrush.

Delgany Golf Club in County Wicklow was founded in 1908. The course was designed by Tom Hood, professional at Royal Dublin. Harry Vardon, a member of the Great Triumvirate and six-times Open champion, remodelled it in 1909. The postcard was posted in that year and illustrates the difficulties lady golfers had to cope with when playing the game (i.e. their long dresses!). It is said that the foundation of Delgany was due to the fact that Sunday golf was not permitted at the nearby Greystones Club.

The Donaghadee Golf Club is situated on the north Down coast and has been in existence since 1899. Few members of the club today would recognise this very large bunker which is faced with the railway sleepers. The clubhouse was built in 1907 and after numerous extensions was completely refurbished in 1992. The eighteen-hole course has several large ditches crossing the fairways. This sandy view would lead one to believe that it is a links course, but it is actually more like parkland.

Uchter John Mark, the 5th Earl of Ranfurly, not only gave Dungannon Golf Club the ground for a twelve-hole course when it was founded in 1890, he was also its first president. His club was a founding member of the Golfing Union of Ireland and he remained president until 1906. The club moved location in 1918 and then again in 1963 when they opened an eighteen-hole course at Mullaghmore.

GOLF HOUSE, DUNMURRY.

The large car parked outside this clubhouse would be an expected sight at this club as it owed its existence largely to leading Belfast industrialists. Founded in 1905, Dunmurry Golf Club has always had problems created by the encroachment of housing and roads around the course. On the original grounds the nine-hole course, designed by H.S. Colt in the late 1920s, was extended to eighteen holes in 1977, but had limited space. In 1982 the course moved to new expansive grounds. Dunmurry's most famous golfer was Max McCready who won the British Amateur Championship at Portmarnock in 1949.

This postcard of Greenore Golf Club was issued by the London & North Western Railway to promote the North Western Hotel at Greenore. Founded in 1896, the course, like many throughout Ireland, owed its origin to the railway. The back of the card advertised 'an excellent eighteen-hole golf course and steamer on Carlingford Lough FREE to visitors staying in the hotel or bungalows.' Other interests mentioned were driving, shooting and sea-fishing. This County Louth course was originally twelve holes, before extending to eighteen in 1897.

Golf Links Greystones
Co Wicklow

Greystones Golf Club in County Wicklow is another club that owes its existence to the railway and a hotel. Golf is said to have been played on this ground in 1892, the first teeing ground being made of concrete with iron posts and connecting chains. The course was extended to eighteen holes in 1914, the new nine holes being laid out by Tom Walker, who was professional from 1906 to 1917. The card shows a graceful ladies' four ball. The clubhouse can be seen in the background. Built in 1896, it was unfortunately recently destroyed by fire.

GOLF CLUB HOUSE, HELEN'S BAY.

Many clubs had small beginnings and their first clubhouses could be very small in comparison to those of today. Both the ladies and men of Helen's Bay shared this one, built a few years after golf had begun there in 1895. The course, which remains one of nine holes, is situated on the shores of Belfast Lough in close proximity to a few other courses, all built on the Dufferin and Ava estate. The head of the Dufferin and Ava family has always been the club's patron or president.

GOLFING AT KILKEE

Kilkee in County Clare was the summer venue for early Limerick golfers before the course at Lahinch was created nearby. Golf was played here as early as 1899. As can be seen in the postcard, the course was laid out along the cliffs. This match seems to have been an important one and among the group young caddies are in evidence. The course moved to its present site at East End in 1937.

Kingstown Golf Club Pavilion.

When this County Dublin golf club was formed in 1909 its first captain was Captain Lionel Hewson, M.V.O. He was a leading golf journalist and established the *Irish Golf* magazine in 1928. When the course was extended to eighteen holes in 1920 Harry Colt, the famous British golf architect, was employed to redesign the course. It was here in 1964 that Tommy Campbell is reputed to have hit the longest recorded drive at that time, measuring 392 yards. This card was posted in 1913 and shows some staff standing beside tables outside a very smart clubhouse. Given other changes which took place in titles throughout the Republic of Ireland, it is surprising that the club did not change its name to Dun Laoghaire Golf Club until 1951.

Posted in June 1938 this postcard of the clubhouse at Kirkistown Castle Golf Club near Cloughey, County Down, shows it bedecked in flags, probably for the Coronation of George VI. The club was formed in 1902 and the course is situated close to the coast. On a good day there are views across the Irish Sea to the Isle of Man, but on a bad day the wind can cause problems for the golfers driving from the elevated tees.

Golf Club House, Knock Golf Club.

Knock Golf Club was one of the earliest golf courses in Belfast. Like many city courses it has been forced to move several times since it was formed in 1895. This clubhouse was at the second location in the Shandon Park Estate. The club moved here in 1898, remaining until 1920 when it moved to its present site at Summerfield. This house still stands on the boundary of Shandon Park Golf Club which took over the old course. This card was posted in 1914.

This card posted in 1906 shows the first clubhouse at the world-famous Lahinch Golf Club. This is the home of the South of Ireland Championship which dates back to 1895. John Burke, a Lahinch member, won this championship no less than ten times. Members of Limerick Golf Club and the Blackwatch Regiment were both responsible for the early development of the eighteen-hole course.

The Dell, Golf Links, Lahinch. Co. Clare

This card gives a very good view of the sand hills and the impact they had on this County Clare links course. This hole, 'The Dell', has great significance in that it is all that remains of the design laid out by the 'Great Old Man of Golf', Tom Morris. After an initial course had been marked out in 1892, Tom Morris redesigned it in 1894. In 1904 Charles Gibson of Westward Ho changed the layout to incorporate more of the sand hills. Then in 1927 Dr Alister Mackenzie, who had designed the Augusta National and Cypress Point, was called in to modernise the links. It could hardly fail to be a great golf course after such a pedigree.

Golf Links Hotel, Lahinch, Co. Clare.

This card, posted in 1914, illustrates the importance of both the hotel and the railway in the early development of golf courses, especially those in more remote regions. The railway which served Lahinch was the West Clare Railway which was the subject of a song by the Irish songwriter Percy French. The fine hotel was constructed totally of wood, but was destroyed by fire in 1934.

GOLF PAVILION, ISLANDMAGEE.

This clubhouse on Islandmagee belongs to Larne Golf Club which was founded in 1894. At that time the course was reached by a ferry which left from Larne Harbour and which was connected to the railway network. The ferry fare was one penny. The *Irish Golfer 1900* describes this building as 'a neat commodious clubhouse'.

Lisburn Golf Club was formed in 1891 when play began on the Manor House Park. At that time a major problem facing many inland courses was the lack of equipment capable of cutting the grass in the summer and initially this nine-hole course was only open for play from November to April. The clubhouse pictured was practically in the centre of the town and it was inevitable that the club had to move to another site. They moved to a new course, designed by the golf architect Fred Hawtree, on the outskirts of Lisburn in 1973.

Golf Links, Malahide, Co. Dublin.

The Malahide Golf Club in County Dublin began in 1892. The course, like many which are situated right beside the sea, has suffered from coastal erosion and has had to retreat on a number of occasions. The club now has a new twenty-seven hole complex, designed by Ireland's most prolific golf course architect, the late Eddie Hackett.

Malone Golf Club in Belfast showed great foresight when they built this clubhouse in 1897. The well-known architect Harold Seaver was asked to design it so that it could easily be converted to a private dwelling should the club decide to move. It was built at a cost of £900. At this time the course was just a short tram ride from the centre of the city. By 1913 the course was too small and the club moved to a new site. They moved again in 1962 to their present course at Ballydrain. The present clubhouse was built in 1835 and was home to a family in the linen industry. The building pictured is still a beautiful dwelling house.

Golfing on Lough Neagh Links, Antrim. RELIABLE SERIES

Massereene Golf Club, established in 1895, plays on a course at Antrim which was built right on the shores of Lough Neagh on grounds provided by Lord Massereene, the 11th Viscount Massereene, who was the club's first president. It was a nine-hole course until 1961 when F.W. Hawtree designed a new, larger course. The clubhouse in the postcard is part of the professional's shop today. Note the hole-marker by the caddie in the centre (which was not a flag), and also the dress of the golfers and caddies. This card was posted in 1913.

The famous Irish amateur golfer James Bruen always listed Muskerry as his home club. When he won the British Boys' Amateur Championship in 1935, he became the first person to win a championship organised by the Royal and Ancient Golf Club. He was only fifteen years of age. In addition to winning the Irish Amateur, he also won the British Amateur Championship in 1939. This club had a slightly chequered early history. It was founded in 1897 as the Muskerry Golf and Lawn Tennis Club, but this was short-lived. Another club, St Ann's Hill, was formed in 1902 and the Muskerry Club was re-established in 1907; the two clubs then merged around 1910. Alister Mackenzie designed the course.

Lisfannon Golf Links, Buncrana Co. Donegal.

The North-West Golf Club at Lisfannon, founded in 1891, was one of that select group of clubs to form the Golfing Union of Ireland that same year. The other clubs were the County Club (later Royal Portrush), County Down, Aughnacloy, Ballycastle, Dungannon, Killymoon, Portsalon, and Royal Belfast. The two golfers pictures have caddies, albeit of differing ages. Before the use of any form of trolley this would have been very common. The large box on the teeing ground is the sand box, from which the golfer, or his caddie, would make a 'tee' upon which to place the ball before driving. Lionel Munn, a member of the club, was Ireland's first truly great golfer, winning a hat-trick of Irish Open Amateur Championship titles from 1909 to 1911. This is the first tee, with the railway line to nearby Buncrana in the background.

This card, posted in Rathmullen in 1908, gives a fascinating insight into early golf. Golf is reputed to have been played here as early as the 1850s by British Army officers stationed in the Martello Tower shown in the picture. While there is doubt about the actual date, the club affiliated to the Golfing Union of Ireland around 1893. The course's difficult terrain can clearly be seen. Grazing livestock, whether they were sheep or cattle, were used to keep the grass under control. On many courses greens had wires around them to keep the animals off the putting surface, not that they were the closely mown greens of today.

This card showing the course of Portsalon, posted in 1903, gives a good idea of the nature of the golf to be found on this part of the coast of Donegal. Portsalon Golf Club was one of the nine founder members of the Golfing Union of Ireland in 1891, just a few months after the formation of the club. The hickory-shafted golf clubs must have suffered some damage when playing among these rocky parts. Lost golf balls were most likely a major problem as well.

Work began at the Strand or West Course at Portstewart as early as 1908. Willie Park, the famous Scottish professional, gave it his attention in 1913 and such was the quality of the early design that only minor changes took place prior to its expansion in the mid-1960s. The clubhouse pictured in this card was opened in 1928 when two top amateurs Cyril Tolley and Charles Hezlet played with two local professionals in an exhibition match. In 1986 the decision was taken to incorporate more true links, and the 'Thistly Hollow Project' began. The new course was ready for the Irish Close Championship in 1992.

THE HOME GREEN, ROSAPENNA.

R. WELCH.

This appears to have been an important match finishing on the final green of the course at Rosapenna, with the hotel close by. This excellent piece of golfing ground is said to have been discovered accidentally by Tom Morris around 1891. Other course designers to give it their attention were Harry Vardon and James Braid, who with J.H. Taylor made up 'the Great Triumvirate', winning sixteen Open championships between them from 1894 to 1914. Eddie Hackett was responsible for the most recent design of this County Donegal course.

Rosslare Golf Club is another club that owes its existence to private initiative. It is rare to find a postcard which features an amateur golf championship and this one commemorates the Irish Close Championship of 1934. In over one hundred years of the championship, this was the only time it was played at Rosslare. The winner was J.C. Brown of Waterford who beat R.M. McConnell of Royal Portrush. Another unmistakable figure is that of Cecil Ewing of County Sligo, standing on the right in the top right picture. The top centre photograph is of the Knock Golf Club Junior Cup team, All-Ireland winners in 1934.

This card, posted in 1907, shows Carnalea Golf Club. The Royal Belfast Golf Club moved to this site after they had to leave their original course at The Kinnegar. Founded in 1881, the club is recognised as the first formal golf club in Ireland. They moved to Carnalea in 1892 and remained there until 1925. A founder member of the Golfing Union of Ireland, the club provided its first officers. In 1885 the club became entitled to use the prefix 'Royal' when the Prince of Wales became patron.

Craigavad House from the Avenue.

The Royal Belfast Golf Club purchased Craigavad House and its estates in 1925. It was built by Lord Dunleath in 1881 and cost the club all of £6,000. The members contributed £11,500 in debentures towards the cost of converting it into a clubhouse and building the golf course. H.S. Colt designed the course and it has magnificent views over Belfast Lough. George L. Baillie, one of the club's founding members, was instrumental in laying out many early courses all over Ireland. Sir James Henderson played a vital part in the club's development. As owner of the *Belfast Newsletter*, one of Ireland's oldest newspapers, he did much to promote the game of golf throughout Ireland.

Golf Links, Newcastle, Co Down

The County Down Club, Newcastle, was instituted in 1889, the fourth club in Ulster, and was a founder member of the Golfing Union of Ireland. Tom Morris of St Andrews visited the course in 1889 and laid out the links on instruction from the club council at 'an expense not to exceed £4'. This card, posted in 1916, shows the captain, Fred H. Rogers, 'driving himself into office'. The magnificent clubhouse opened in 1897 and is still in use today. To the left of the clubhouse, railway carriages can be seen which shows the close proximity of the railway platform. 'Golfer's Express' trains were a feature of the early development of the club which was granted royal patronage in 1908, becoming Royal County Down. The club has hosted many local championships, the British Amateur Championship, the Curtis Cup, and more recently the Senior British Open Championship.

From the beginning of golf in Ireland nearly all clubs welcomed ladies as members, but only a few, such as Royal County Down, were able to offer them their own course and clubhouse (Royal Portrush was another). This card depicts the final of the Irish Ladies' Close Championship of 1902, played on the main course at Royal County Down. Good crowds were in attendance.

This wonderful wooden clubhouse at Royal Dublin was the result of extensions to the original one which was built in 1899. Unfortunately it suffered the fate of many such clubhouses, being destroyed by fire in 1943. The smaller building is the professional's shop of Tom Hood. He was professional from 1896 to 1914. On the postcard one can read the adverts for Kite golf balls on the windows of the shop. Dublin Golf Club began its life in Phoenix Park where it is said that Scottish regiments played golf in the 1850s. The club was founded in 1885, the third to be formed in Ireland. The club moved to Dollymount in 1889. In 1921 H.S. Colt redesigned the course and it has maintained its prominence as one of the leading golf clubs in Ireland.

Golf House, Portrush.

The County Club at Portrush was formed in 1888. By 1892 the membership had grown to 370 and it had become the Royal County Club; it became the Royal Portrush Golf Club in 1895. Portrush was another founding member of the Golfing Union of Ireland, all the founding clubs being in Ulster. This card, posted in 1927, shows the clubhouse which was built in 1892. Portrush has hosted all the important Irish championships, both ladies' and men's. It remains the only course outside of Great Britain to host the Open Championship, which it did in 1951. Max Faulkner was the winner. Fred Daly, Ireland's only Open champion, began his golfing career as a caddie on these famous links.

ROYAL PORTRUSH GOLF LINKS.
MANN'S BUNKER. *LEE.*

This photograph was taken during the 1903 British Ladies' Championship. The finalists were Rhona Adair and May Hezlet, both members of Royal Portrush. They are seen playing the twelfth hole and negotiating Mann's Bunker, '150 yards long with railway sleepers along the back'. Rhona Adair won this championship, repeating her win of 1900. She also won the Irish Ladies' Championship four years running from 1900 to 1903. May Hezlet won the British Ladies' Championship three times (in 1899, 1902, and 1907), and the Irish Championship five times (in 1899, from 1904 to 1906, and in 1908).

Many Irish golf courses were created with the assistance of Scottish professionals. Among these was Old Tom Morris who laid out well-known courses such as those at Royal County Down, Lahinch and Rosapenna. The professionals also played in exhibition matches. On one occasion Tom Morris played a match at Royal County Down on the Wednesday, played the return match at Royal Portrush on the Thursday, inspected the new nine-hole course there on the Friday, and later that day boarded the steamer back to Scotland. He then played a match at St Andrews on the Saturday. This was in 1889 when he was sixty-eight years old! In the background of the picture is the shed for the Giant's Causeway tram.

Scrabo Golf Links, Club House and Tower, nr. Newtownards.

The game of 'goff' had been referred to in the Newtownards area in the early part of the seventeenth century. However, the modern game did not begin there until the course at Scrabo opened in 1908. G.L. Baillie, formerly of Musselburgh and a founder of Royal Belfast Golf Club, was paid the grand sum of two guineas to lay out the course in what can only be described – due to its hilltop situation – as an area not totally suited to golf! In 1971, the club somehow found additional ground to increase to the course to eighteen holes.

The Ulster Spa was situated just outside the town of Ballynahinch in County Down and was the only one in the province. It was thought that the game of golf would be an added attraction for those 'taking the waters'. It is no surprise to learn that a local hotelier was one of the prime movers. The course was a short one, with the longest hole just 230 yards. Surprisingly, it was not until 1967 that the Spa Golf Club moved to another nine-hole course, which was actually closer the town. This has subsequently been extended to eighteen holes.

Golf Links, Spa, Ballynahinch.

Golf Pavilion, Strabane.

Strabane Golf Club was instituted in 1909, the course being close to the centre of town. Like many inland courses in the early 1900s it was a winter course only. The club moved to its present course at Ballycolman in 1953 and extended to an eighteen-hole course in 1974.

Sutton Golf Club (left) is the home club of Ireland's most famous amateur golfer, the great Joe Carr. He won the British Amateur Championship three times. Cush Point, site of this nine-hole golf course, is another of the oldest golfing sites in Ireland. At one time in 1888 Dublin Golf Club considered moving to this area, before deciding on Dollymount. The Dublin Scottish Golf Club played here, before the Sutton Boat and Yacht Golf Club was formed in 1896 (this name was retained until 1900). This card was posted in 1956. Caddies were still in use at that time, although it was not long before caddie-carts were introduced.

Whitehead Golf Club in County Antrim is typical of many early clubs in that its founders had difficulty in determining which was the best site. Founded in 1904, the first course was close to the station, but by 1909 the course had moved to land owned by the Marquis of Donegall. It remained there until 1936 when it returned to the original site, becoming a nine-hole course designed by James Braid. Braid, who was Open Champion five times, was by this time sixty-six and it must have been one of his last designs. Finally the club moved to a new eighteen-hole course in 1974.

THE CLIFFS FROM GOLF LINKS, WICKLOW.

Many Irish golf courses are fortunate to have coastal settings and some of them are among the best links courses in the world. Wicklow Golf Club is still a nine-hole course set on the high lying coast towards Wicklow Head. The cliff tops were originally covered in deep furze and took a long time to clear. To avoid losing balls a fore-caddie was often employed. The course was laid out in 1904 by Tom Hood, professional at Royal Dublin from 1896 to 1914. This card was posted in 1934.